UNDERSTANDING THE DOG'S MIND

Through Survival & Comfort

CALVIN WILBON

THE CHOICE
PUBLISHING HOUSE

The Choice Publishing House
1910 Madison Avenue #2385
Memphis, TN 38104
www.thechoicepublishinghouse.com
(901) 443-7338

First published by The Choice Publishing House 03/26/2021

ISBN: 978-0-578-87755-6

Library of Congress Control Number: 2021905417

Printed in the United States of America

The publisher and the author make no guarantees concerning the level of success you may experience by following the advice and strategies contained in this book, and you accept the risk that results will differ for each individual. The testimonials and examples provided in this book show exceptional results, which may not apply to the average reader, and are not intended to represent or guarantee that you will achieve the same or similar results.

Because of the dynamic of the Internet, any Web addresses or links contained or mentioned in this book may have changed since publication and may no longer be valid. The views expressed in this work are solely those of the author and do not necessarily reflect the views of the publisher, and the publisher hereby disclaims any responsibility for them.

MISSION STATEMENT

MY PASSION IS TO MAKE LIFE BETTER FOR DOGS. Every year, nearly 700,000 dogs are put down in shelters in the United States alone, many of which are there because they are considered "lost causes." In fact, the majority of these dogs are who they are because of an owner who didn't know how to communicate with them or understand what leads a dog down the wrong path in life.

The purpose behind writing this book is to educate dog owners which, will have a direct impact on reducing the number of dogs that find themselves in kill shelters simply because their mind was not trained in the right way.

We are the reason our dogs view life the way they do, either the right way or the wrong way. As much as we try to figure our dog out, the dog is trying just as hard to figure us out as well. In fact, they don't ever stop trying to figure us out, so it's up to us to understand every step we take in this special relationship leaves a footprint on the dog's behavior. Dog owners must be aware that they are constantly training the dog's mind and must do so intentionally and consistently.

This book will explain the depth of knowledge that goes into owning a dog, how to understand current behaviors and how to prevent bad behaviors. With this understanding, we can greatly reduce the number of strays, pound dogs and those "behavior" that we have now. In the process, we can create happy, well-adjusted pets who provide lifelong enjoyment and companionship.

If you are reading this, you care about your dog, and for that I thank you. As much as I want to educate you, my real mission in this project is to help improve the quality of life for your pet. After all, dogs don't choose their owners. Owners choose their dogs. My mission—and promise—is to help dog lovers all around the world understand the way a dog thinks and reacts to life!

FOREWORD

I WOULD LIKE TO THANK GOD BECAUSE I WENT TO HIM with a burning desire and asked Him to help me understand this animal on another level. He brought that to fruition. I also have to thank my parents for raising this country boy and putting me in a situation to witness the most natural way a dog lives. Also, many thanks to my partner Cecil Brannon for introducing me to the business world of dog training. I'm so thankful for my village.

CONTENTS

INTRODUCTION

Many of us are inseparable from our dogs, and it is easy to see why. They provide us with companionship, with comfort in difficult times, and give us an outlet for the need we humans have to care for another living thing. Nobody who ever owned a dog ever grew tired of seeing that animal greet them after a long day of work, playing fetch for hours, or being there when we need them most.

I know what that feels like because I have been a dog person for as long as I can remember. My mom tells me that the toys I went to as a baby were always stuffed animals, and other family members recall how fascinated I was with the first live dog I remember – Toby, a German shepherd mix – that came into my life when I was around three years old.

Toby introduced me to the joy a dog can bring, and I spent many hours playing with him and being around him. I also remember how much it hurt when he broke his leash and took off, never to be seen again. While he didn't stay in my life for long, Toby made me understand how deep the bond between animal and human goes and how quickly it forms. Toby running away brought me to the realization that dogs don't only seek love in life. There has to be more to it.

I have owned many dogs since Toby and trained hundreds in my career. With each one of them, the goal has been the same: To better understand the mind of the animal, its natural instincts, and to shape those natural instincts to learn and cope with everyday life. And that is what this book is all about.

Training a dog is impossible without first understanding the dog, and by that, I mean knowing its nature as a species and as an individual animal. No two dogs are exactly alike, but they are all ruled by certain basic motivations. The dog owner – or trainer, for that matter – who doesn't understand this fact will not have long-term success in training the animal. You can't win against nature, but you can (and must) use it to your advantage.

As you read through this book, you will likely come across facts that will challenge your beliefs about your relationship with your dog. But they are just that – facts – things I have learned through more than a decade of working with all shapes, sizes and temperaments of canines. My training system doesn't rely on emotion, it deals with the cause-and-effect, real-world facts of life that drive a dog's behavior and its view of the world. And it works.

THE HARDEST LESSON TO LEARN

No one would try to train their child as a monkey or approach a lion like a housecat because logic tells you they aren't the same creature;

they have different motivations and intentions, and therefore have to be handled differently.

Dogs have to be approached the same way. You can't treat dogs like four-legged humans. Nature didn't set them up that way. You have to approach them according to how the dog sees life and the world around them. The bottom line is, humans have to approach human-canine relationships the way the canine perceives the relationship and not the other way around.

Fortunately, humans have been blessed with an intellect that allows us to understand this viewpoint, and with proper study and practice, we learn how to manipulate a dog's motivations to behave in a certain way. In other words, we have dominion over the animal. We are told in Genesis 1:26: *"And God said, 'Let us make man in our image, according to our likeness; and let them have dominion over the fish of the sea and over the birds of the air, and over all the wild animals of the earth, and over every creeping thing that creeps upon the earth.'*

And so, what are the facts of life when it comes to a dog's view of the world? It's actually pretty simple – Dogs see everything in one of two categories, survival and comfort. That's it. Everything a dog sees, does or experiences, it evaluates based on these two criteria, and it will choose actions that maximize its chance of survival and level of comfort.

Now you're saying to yourself: "That doesn't seem too hard to get my head around," and it's not. But what if I told you that the dog you love so much doesn't really love you back, at least not in the human sense of the word? What if I told you that the things you think the dog is doing out of love, or loyalty, or to please you, really all come down to a handful of kibble?

Dogs can be trained to do remarkable things. In police and military applications, they can be taught to do things that seem to contradict the laws of survival and nature. But they don't do it "just because." An owner should not think for a second a police or military dog is performing out of duty or patriotism or that the family pet sits and stays for the pride of a job well done. Those are human emotions, and they really are meaningless concepts in the mind of a dog.

The good news is that a dog's nature can be harnessed in such a way that the dog believes that doing their job – even a dangerous, potentially life-threatening job – is actually their best chance for survival and comfort. They have been trained to understand that following a command or performing a task is the best and most efficient way to satisfy their natural behavioral instincts. And because they have those instincts, it gives us the chance to build their training on the things they value most.

This is generally very, very difficult for the typical dog owner to understand because they want to assign human feelings to a non-human creature and try to train them that way. That thinking is doomed to failure when it comes to dogs because you're expecting an animal to think and feel like a person. It's the same as comparing a house cat to a lion.

One example I like to give to clients is to imagine you've been abducted by space aliens. Nothing looks familiar, you don't know what you can eat or when, you can't understand the language, and all you really want to know is how you will survive and keep from being hurt. You don't love the aliens, but you need them to accomplish this goal. So, they start assigning you tasks, and when you're praised or rewarded with food for doing something right, you repeat that behavior. You do it because you know it gets you what you need, not because it makes you feel good about yourself or out of any sense of loyalty. You're just trying to survive and stay comfortable. That, in a nutshell, is a dog's daily reality.

This is, without question, the hardest lesson for dog owners to come to terms with. But once you do, you'll find that you see your dog in a whole different light, and you'll start to recognize the cause-and-effect relationship that rules your dog's behavior. You'll start to see how the animal really sees you: as the source of everything that they value. And you will learn how to use these natural instincts to develop the dog's behaviors.

SEEK PROFESSIONAL HELP

It's equally important to remember that even if you accept every word in this book, it does not replace the effect that a skilled and experienced trainer will have on your animal. Dog trainers, the good ones, have honed their understanding and technique for training dogs just like the best doctors, lawyers, and other professionals have done in their professions.

Think about it: If you accidentally cut yourself in the kitchen, you could research a solution, and you could probably even perform some first aid to keep from bleeding out or getting an infection. But sooner or later, 99 percent of us are going to find our way to a trained medical professional to provide real medical care, probably sooner rather than later. And when we get that medical attention, and we're told what to do once we get back home to promote healing, chances are we do it.

Well, in a perfect world, that's how dog training is supposed to work. But too often, people get a dog and read an article, see a video or just try to follow common sense to train it, only to get frustrated when the dog doesn't respond. Or, they'll seek out a trainer like myself, pay money for my expertise and services, and then fail to consistently do the "follow-up treatment," allowing the dog to go back to bad habits. What dog owners need to understand is that there is a difference between behaviors and obedience. Behaviors can be viewed as tricks (i.e., sit, stand, come), but true obedience is how they conduct themselves in a given setting.

A quality dog trainer practices his or her craft 24/7/365 and immerses the animal during the training process. This is different from a dog owner, who has a lot of things pulling at their attention span in daily life. Good trainers are consistent as well as knowledgeable; they approach training as an art, a science and a business and therefore pay their full attention to the job in front of them. And most of all, the best trainers never stop learning.

Any dog trainer who tells you they know absolutely everything about dogs isn't telling you the truth. I have built a successful business on a track record of quality work, spread out over hundreds of animals from household pets to elite protection animals, and I still don't know everything there is to know. But what I have done is cracked the code on the foundational elements of canine instinct and motivation. It is from that foundation that I can address a dog's individual quirks or issues.

The result? I have been tremendously successful in developing well-trained dogs consistently. You may be asking yourself, if a trainer is the best way to get results, then why read this book in the first place? Remember a second ago when we were at the doctor's, and they told you the medical treatment to do at home? Chances are they told you why – how the treatment works, its contraindications, and what to look out for that could disrupt the healing process.

Well, reading this book will give you that same kind of insight, helping you relate to your dog appropriately so that old, bad habits do not return and new bad habits don't form.

Remember: As good as I am at what I do, as a trainer, I am only as effective as you allow me to be *after* your dog comes home. This book will put you in a better position to be an effective partner in your dog's training and performance, thus affecting your quality of life as well as your pet's.

Let's get started!

CHAPTER 1
COMFORT

If we could somehow get into a time machine and transport back through history, back before humans had come up with civilizations, science and technology, back to a time when you could only eat what you could hunt or gather, we would have a much better understanding of how a dog sees life.

That's because primitive humans – let's call them cavemen – hadn't yet developed the ability to think on a higher level. Prehistoric humans didn't worry about where their career was going, they didn't wonder if their latest tweet was going viral, and they didn't dream about what they were going to be when they grew up. The biggest ambition they had was to deal with what was in front of them in a way that didn't get them eaten or hurt.

As humans, we have become more "civilized," but dogs have remained in this mindset, unchanged, for thousands of years. Before dogs were domesticated, they woke up and did what they had to do to survive and stay comfortable doing it. These two motivations are not mutually exclusive: A dog will develop strategies for its survival that are more efficient and more direct. In other words, what "shortcuts" can I take that delivers maximum food for minimal risk or effort?

All living creatures are geared, fundamentally, in achieving and maintaining comfort. Humans are the only beings that will voluntarily go against nature and do things the "hard way" or go "above and beyond" out of personal satisfaction or to get ahead in life. All other members of the animal kingdom are looking to satisfy their instinctual drive while sacrificing as little for their comfort as they can, and still get the job done.

Think about a wolf, one of the most powerful and ferocious beasts of the wild, blessed with the strength, speed and stamina to take down almost any prey it can find. Given a choice between taking on healthy adult prey and hunting down animals that are weaker, such as a baby or an older animal, they will take the obvious, most advantageous choice every time. And why? Same payoff for less effort and less chance of taking an antler to the guts.

Dogs still have that basic problem-solving mentality: How do I get what I want with a minimum amount of discomfort? But as we've moved dogs into domesticated environments, the picture becomes more complicated. Dogs don't see your house as you do. To them, it's no different than the great outdoors. For example, if you had a tree growing in the middle of your living room, your dog wouldn't be fazed as you would. At the same time, the dog has to play by the human's rules, and that means it can no longer do what's most direct – for instance, snatch a plate of food off the counter or relieve themselves anywhere they like in the house.

This is the essence of effective dog training – to set in the animal's mind that the quickest and easiest way to get what they want is to act in a certain way, as triggered by a given command. A dog's instincts are intact from the moment it's born, but can be shaped dramatically. It's particularly effective when dealing with puppies, because they don't have a "track record" of doing things on their own. If shown right from wrong from the jump, they don't have any reason to try and figure out other ways to get what they want.

And, unlike humans who are always trying to build a better mousetrap, once I teach a puppy a successful way of doing things, they don't try to improve on it. It doesn't dawn on them to seek an alternative unless I give them a reason to or let them think they can find a "better way."

With puppies, I have all knowledge of what that puppy has witnessed or hasn't. Puppies are a blank slate, which is why when it comes to raising them, I make sure that, if I'm not there to stop or influence behavior – in other words, if I'm not actively working with them – then the puppy is put up in its crate. A puppy is always learning, so I don't want it to witness bad habits on its own.

Dogs don't fully develop mentally until they're three, three and a half years old. If a dog is three and a half or older, you can almost be certain that whatever behaviors that dog has witnessed throughout its life have almost become permanent. It's living almost entirely by the programming it has had in life.

Now let me say right here: Age alone doesn't mean that the dog is a goner, but the age of a dog does change the intensity and length of the training. An adult dog has a lot of reps in being the way that it is. If you adopt an adult dog, you don't necessarily know what went on in its life that triggered it to do certain things. You get the whole package, the good and the bad, but that doesn't mean you're stuck with the bad. Dogs adapt and evolve, or they wouldn't be dogs.

SHOW ME WHAT WORKS

So, how do you teach the correct behavior, or change undesirable behaviors, with a creature that doesn't think like you do or literally doesn't speak your language? Well, that's one of the great things about dogs as a species: They are very result-oriented. A key thing to remember about dogs is, they're not going to keep trying something time after time if it doesn't pay off.

Let me give you an example: Let's say that I've got a food bowl, and every time that dog goes to the food bowl, a lid closes. The dog tries to bite at it. It won't open. The dog tries to claw at it. It won't open. The dog will finally leave it alone. No matter how hungry that dog gets, if that lid closes every time it approaches and opens every time it leaves, that dog has already learned, "I've tried this, it doesn't work."

In fact, and this is the amazing part about a dog's thinking, if you do this long enough, the dog will eventually get to a point where it will ignore a full food bowl that's sitting out in the open because, in their mind, they're thinking, "Aha! I know this trick. As soon as I get up and get over there, the lid's gonna close. I'm not falling for that again."

Or, if you've ever seen a wild animal try to bite an armadillo, you know that in most cases, the armadillo will roll up in a ball to protect its soft underbelly, leaving only its hard shell exposed. A dog will quickly give up on that to go hunt other prey, because trying to bite the armadillo isn't working.

So, what does that mean for you as a dog owner? It is vitally important that you demonstrate to your dog the easiest way to get what they want and maintain their comfort is to follow your rules. In this manner, you, the dog owner, present the most effective way to accomplish this goal.

Now, I hear you out there: "That's it? That's the big secret? Shoot, Calvin, **what do you think I've been trying to do?**" Well, like anything else, understanding a concept and putting it into practice effectively are two very, very different things. When I tell people about a dog's comfort drive, most of them get it right away, because it holds up to logic. But putting it to work as part of a dog's training is not so easy.

BE THE BOSS, HUMAN!

Part of what makes this so tough for a lot of people is because they are not committed to acting like the boss at all times. Let's say you have a dog that barks constantly. As a human, you might be tempted to give the dog a rawhide to chew on because you know if it is chewing, it will stop the barking. But what have you really done? You've let the dog know, "Hey, if I bark enough, I get a treat."

Or, let's say you're trying to get the dog to stay. You get it to sit, you back up, and the dog gets up. You make them sit again, you back up, and the same thing happens. After a while, you get tired and a little frustrated, but you still want the dog to know you love them, so you give them a treat for a "nice try." Well, dogs don't understand "participation ribbons!" You've just told them what they were doing was all it takes to get what they want.

This is another byproduct of treating your dog like you would your child – we do this to our kids all the time either to promote self-esteem or to get some peace and quiet, knowing that as the child grows and matures, we have time to shape behavior. And, because the child will develop language and reasoning skills, we can explain our actions or later lay down the law verbally.

Dogs don't have those kinds of cognitive skills. Even in the case of elite dogs, dogs with dangerous jobs in stressful environments that put them in harm's way, they have been trained to the point that they are convinced that whatever they are asked to do is the shortest and most effective means of maintaining comfort.

So how do we do this? First, get your priorities straight. One of the things I always say is, "Train first and then have a pet later." You want to make sure that you instill all the things in this dog's mind to make it a confident dog in the end. It's all about associations; if you know how to control associations, then the dog can be raised to where you can have the dog that you want and be able to do the things that you want to do.

With any training program, the first step is establishing a value system. The extent that a dog values something will dictate what you can convince it to do in terms of behavior. Treats are really good for associations. Use that treat as a high-value reward and time it for when the dog is displaying good behavior. Give your dog a treat if they're sitting on command. Give your dog a treat if they're showing any type of behavior that you like on command. If you're housebreaking a dog, give it a treat for peeing or pooping outside. That's reinforcement; the dog values the treat, and the behavior becomes associated with the treat. The rest is consistent repetition.

It should be noted that good behavior should not only be rewarded "on command," but spontaneous obedience should also be rewarded from a young age. Giving a treat "just because" is a mistake people make all the time. Dogs can do good things by accident. Use these moments as a reward opportunity to encourage good behaviors. Then, capitalize off of it.

Always remember, you want the command, the action, and the treat to come in that order. This keeps it clear in the dog's mind that they only get rewarded for following a specific command. Otherwise, you're working against yourself.

You can also transition a dog from the learning phase to the reinforcement phase of their training by some other signal. For me, I am a big believer in using a clicker. While a dog is learning a skill where they are getting rewarded, click the clicker. The dog will begin to associate that behavior equals the click, and the click results in a treat. So, when you move into daily reinforcement, the behavior equals the click. "I hear the click," says the dog, "that's my notification for a job well done."

I like to use the example that the click is like hearing a notification on your phone that you got a text message, the text message being the actual food. Eating and swallowing the food is equivalent to reading the text message. Then, the message is received.

CONSISTENCY IS KEY

Again, I cannot stress enough how important consistency is to the overall success of training—or maintaining the training—of your dog. In physics there are two opposing forces: the irresistible force and the immovable object. You have to be the immovable object who will only accept correct behavior, no matter how long you have to stand there to get it.

I always tell my clients, "If the dog gets it wrong 100 times, you have to be willing to correct it 101 times." Anything less, and you're sending the wrong message, reinforcing the wrong behavior and working against yourself. The most important thing you can learn from this book is, you are always training your dog, either consciously or subconsciously, whether you know it or not. If you accept less than what you're asking for, you're basically allowing the lifestyle and environment to train the dog for you.

The other thing that you have to develop in the dog when you're talking about comfort is trust. The dog has to trust that you are leading it to a place that will be comfortable, no matter what they have to do to get there. A dog will do something they ordinarily would not do if they believe it's the price to pay for getting what they want. Every one of the dogs I have trained—and especially the dogs I have owned personally—knows me as the source of their primary comfort. They trust that there's a reward coming somewhere in the process, even if that reward is just feelings of comfort and safety.

I have a dog right now named Primo, and he's one of the best dogs I've ever had. He's about as well-trained as a dog can get. People are amazed at how he will just stare at me. Dogs in general will come up to him and bark at him - this is a distraction. He may glance at them, but then he's staring at me. If he's doing obedience drills, he just stares at me. If there's another dog in the vicinity, he doesn't care. He doesn't care that it's a male. He doesn't care that it's a female. It's about me. We have a relationship where I control his comfort and survival, and because of that, I can introduce him to the world.

Recently, we flew on an airplane, something he isn't familiar with. I was extremely happy with how he took it, because he did not freak out or do anything out of discomfort. At the airport, he also went on an escalator for the first time, and he took it like a champ. He did it with a lot of confidence because, when I saw the dog, I saw in his mind that he was saying, "I'm with Calvin, so even though this is unfamiliar, it must be OK."

Now, the facts are, as a trainer, it's not me alone they will trust and obey, but whoever steps into my place. If the dog only listened to me and there was no way to transfer that trust to the owner, I'd be out of business really quick. As a matter of fact, if I gave one of my personal dogs to someone, even Primo, it would be "Calvin who?" a lot quicker than I probably care to admit. But that's how the dog's mind works.

Remember what we said before – dogs don't form relationships in the same way that humans do. They will respond to a new owner that provides their need for survival and comfort just as well as their trainer, provided the owner reinforces the behavior properly.

And that's really where the problems come in. People want to blame the dog for not "remembering" their training when the facts are, the primary reason why they fail is that the person decreased drive or motivation for certain things. My dog Primo can be the most trained dog on Earth, but he can go somewhere else and change. That's how they operate. It's what people allow of the dog.

In all honesty, you have all control over the dog's life. People will sometimes blame genetics for a dog's actions. Depending on how the dog reacts and recovers from experiences, will determine genetics or just the lack of experience. As the trainer, it's my job to bring certain things out of a dog, and as the owner, it's your job to keep them at the forefront.

CHOOSING THE RIGHT PUPPY

I get it – all puppies are cute. Essentially, any puppy can be trained, but all puppies are not created equal. When picking out your puppy, there are certain characteristics and personality traits that give you an idea of the dog they will grow into. Even though they can't talk, a puppy will tell you a lot about itself just by its body language. Here are some things to look for:

1. As a general rule, I don't like a puppy that has its tail down, runs up to me, wants to jump on me and in between my legs because it shows me that the dog is going to be the one that forms separation anxiety.

2. By the same token, the puppy that's standoffish and doesn't necessarily know what a human is, that's maybe looking at you crazy, or with every move that you make, it looks like it wants to leave; nine times out of ten, that's the puppy you don't want.

3. You want an independent puppy. Look for a puppy that knows that you're there and will come up to you, but it's willing to leave you to go do whatever it wants to do. Look for a puppy whose tail is up, that jumps around every now and then and gets these little

bursts of energy. That means the dog is pushing the environment; it's not letting the environment push it around.

4. I want a puppy that's able to be away from me, but I want a puppy that acknowledges me and knows that I'm there. If it knows that I'm there, it means that it's not afraid of people. If it's comfortable going away from me, that means that it's not as dependent on people.

5. Think about your lifestyle and how a dog fits into that. You don't want to raise your puppy outside of the consistency of your life, one that can't be alone for even a short while without whining and trying to get out of its kennel. The end goal is to have a confident dog, not one who can't be without you.

For example: let's say two puppies were walking out in the woods and a tree fell. Puppy A stops, stares for a long time, maybe even growls or woofs at the fallen trunk. Puppy B hears and sees the tree fall, even feels the vibration it makes when it hits the ground. Shortly after that, the puppy takes off, seemingly forgetting what just happened.

Which puppy do you want?

Most people would choose Puppy A, but it would actually be the lesser choice. In this example, Puppy A is the one showing signs of not being able to deal with environmental stressors, fixating on the fallen tree as if wondering if the tree will make another move. In this state of mind, it will be hard to convince the puppy to do anything other than worry about the tree.

Puppy B, on the other hand, is a good choice because it showed the ability to learn that even when startling things happen, it doesn't last for a long time, and it is okay to continue with the task at hand.

CHAPTER 2

DISCOMFORT

As we've just seen in the previous chapter, comfort is an important motivation and building block in the training of your dog. So why would this chapter focus on discomfort?

Because discomfort is not only a powerful motivator for a dog to act in a certain way, it can be harnessed to shape a dog's behavior to the desired effect. In this chapter, we will take a more in-depth look at how to use situations of discomfort to your advantage in training or reinforcing your dog's behavior.

In thinking about the relationship between discomfort and training, consider this:

"Comfort is the natural ability to learn how to be free from pain or

constraint by first experiencing discomfort."

As we have already said, animals will seek to avoid or escape uncomfortable situations whenever possible. When they can't do that, they may try to demonstrate what we humans think of as aggressive behavior. This doesn't mean that the dog is actually being aggressive. It may just be that the animal is expressing its discomfort (or fear) the only way they know how. The same goes for timid or fearful behavior; it might not be the animal's true nature, but it's how they find relief from whatever is discomforting to them.

A dog who displays behaviors or mannerisms associated with discomfort is giving its owner or trainer a lot of information. In some cases, it can show you what the dog has experienced negatively in its past or, in other cases, it can tell you what the dog has yet to experience, as in the case of a puppy. In cases of behavior problems, knowing the signs that a dog is uncomfortable is essential for the trainer to attack the problem at its source.

Too often, pet owners focus on a dog's behavior and not what's making the animal act as it does. They see the dog damage furniture or pull hard on a leash, or bark at the mailman, and they think the dog is doing it for no reason. They think it's misbehaving like a spoiled child, or acting out of aggression or for the sake of just being mean.

Once again, dogs don't do anything without thinking that what they're doing is going to bring them comfort or increase their survival. Often, this is just a reflex reaction. If a person puts two metal can strings in his hand and runs toward the dog, the dog will skedaddle. It would be extremely scared and wouldn't have the guts to even stand its ground.

But if that same dog was cornered or locked in a house with something that was discomforting, it would do whatever it thought best to "make it go away." Take dog bites—the vast majority of dog bites in this country are because the animal weighed all possible reactions and came to the conclusion that the best course of action is to bite. It's not that they're inherently vicious; they're just biting because they're unsure about their situation.

A dog owner—or a trainer, for that matter—has to be able to analyze the animal beyond what they do (behavior) versus what's making them do it (stimulus). They have to be able to go past the dog's action to consider why a certain situation or stimuli is bringing that out of them. Very often, that breaks down to one of the following categories:

1. I don't know what that is.

New experiences can cause a great deal of discomfort for a dog. I worked with a Pitbull once that you wouldn't think would be intimidated by anything, but after a birthday party, he got a hold of a balloon and was playing with it until it popped. It startled him and from that moment on, he wouldn't go near a balloon.

It's very common for dogs of all ages to feel discomfort with things (or people) they don't know. And when they encounter that, they will cycle through their reactions until they find one that works. Without training, that can result in some very bad outcomes, depending on how severe the discomfort, how cornered the dog feels, etc...

2. I've had a bad experience in the past.

I like to say that dogs are smart, but they aren't necessarily intelligent. Where a person knows that each situation is different and should be approached differently, dogs do what feels right to them or what has worked in the past. Left on their own, they will come back to that behavior again and again and again.

People think that if a dog has had a rough background and they're brought into a loving home, the dog's behavior will somehow be magically transformed, as if the dog will automatically "feel the love" and forget everything that happened up to that point. That's simply not the case. And because many people adopt adult and senior dogs, they don't even know what that dog's experience is with this or that. Therefore, they have to pay particular attention to how the dog reacts because even though that's the first time you see your dog in a certain situation, it doesn't mean it's the first time they've been in that situation.

3. I don't trust you to handle it, so I'll handle it.

Remember when we talked about developing trust? Handling new stimuli and unfamiliar experiences are some of the most important moments for doing that. Dog owners shouldn't think that their pet will just get used to something and act right without their participation. You have to play an active role in helping your pet understand they are not in danger and there's nothing to be fearful about. Otherwise, you're at the mercy of how the dog chooses to act, instead of controlling how they act.

If the dog is showing timid-like behavior, then that behavior is going to manifest, and it's going to get worse because that dog feels like this is how it's supposed to live life. Dogs are that simple. However they're living, they're going to continue to live, taking on those behaviors and using their instincts to figure out the situation. As long as I'm surviving by doing this, I'm going to keep doing it every time I'm in this situation.

4. You're the problem, not me.

Dogs think that you should know everything about them and everything about what they're thinking. A dog can see that this human doesn't know much because the energy isn't positive, and some dogs get confused based on the energy. If you don't get in sync with how your dog thinks and therefore dictate the behavior, then the dog will move on to something that is in charge and moving things forward, especially in a situation where they are uncomfortable. That can be another human, that can be another dog (very common), or that can be themselves just demonstrating behavior that they think will fix the issue and bring them comfort.

This doesn't always result in the dog being proactive, confident or strong. Sometimes the dog is reduced to a shaking mess, timid and frightened. I have a lot of clients who bring me their dogs and say, "Well, he's scared of everything." And you can see the dog, crouching with their ears laid back, scared. That's a dog that has learned that it can't count on its human, that they don't have much to do with its survival or comfort. Therefore, it's scared of everything.

Either way, a dog that's been left to figure out how to deal with discomfort on their own will display all kinds of negative behaviors, because this is what they came up with, and they're still alive.

So what do we do to provide comfort? We can't throw out the noisy refrigerator, or stop using the washing machine or tell new people not to come around. We can't eliminate the thousands of things that can startle or make a dog uneasy just because it's new. And as we just saw, we can't just expect the dog to figure it out by themselves because then the dog is telling you how it will behave and not the other way around.

Like a lot of things in this book, the solution is fairly straightforward. As dog owners, we tend to provide comfort in the same moment the dog is uncomfortable, which is wrong. We think this gives the animal the message that there's nothing to fear and that you're in charge of the scary vacuum cleaner or the tennis ball or whatever else has the animal feeling stress. In a sense, you remove the power the object has— the power of the unknown, which is always perceived as a threat—and replace it with your own power in the mind of your animal.

But what the owner should be doing is, in essence, helping the dog understand that the vacuum cleaner and all those "scary objects" are part of its survival. The human needs to turn these situations into positives by proper associations with food. This will, in turn, bring more focus to the owner rather than the object and make them feel more secure with trusting their owner.

Take the example of being locked in a kennel/crate. At first, this can be uncomfortable for a dog, no matter the size or space. A dog is taught to be comfortable in a crate by training its brain to focus on the owner as its source of comfort. As a result, the dog can then view the kennel/crate as good and learn to be comfortable there.

At the heart of all this lies the fact that dogs learn how to control their situation by the feelings it has in that situation and the resulting action it displays. If the dog is unsure about a situation, then, by giving it comfort while uncomfortable, by petting it, you lock that feeling as an association. You want the dog to associate a good feeling of being comfortable even when they are around the thing that makes them uncomfortable.

The end goal is to get the dog to where they don't have to process the situation on their own and decide what to do, because their brain switches over to a comfortable feeling. It's the canine equivalent of "going to my happy place," whenever that clothes dryer or that semi-truck or whatever comes along. A dog can't think about two feelings at once, so the feeling you condition most (which should be positive) is the one they will resort to, their "default setting," if you will.

At the same time, physical contact should be monitored because it could make the dog associate negative feelings, which is discomfort, with gaining comfort/reward from its owner. In that case, you've set in the dog's mind that fear equals reward.

In many cases, it's as simple as providing comfort while the uncomfortable stimuli are going on. Let's say I want to try to get my puppy used to the cardboard box that it is scared of. The second the puppy looks at it, I pet the animal to create good feelings. If I've been using the clicker with the dog to where it knows that the clicker is associated with food, I'll click it to notify the dog that the box is to be associated with something positive. Soon, the clicker will no longer be needed, and the box will become the notification for the reward.

Do this early in the interaction; some owners wait until the puppy goes all the way up to the box and gets startled or scared by it, and then they click to try and undo the discomfort. All you're doing, in that case, is reinforcing what the dog is feeling at the moment (discomfort) with the object, basically defeating your purpose. As soon as the dog sees the box, you should immediately click to cancel the curiosity that it could possibly be a bad thing and harm them, and give them that reinforcing signal that box equals reward.

The way your pet sees it, as long as my owner is consistent and everything else in my environment is consistent, I'm good. When my owner is not consistent, and we don't have a schedule, and you just take me places where my energies are split among each and everything that's out there, that's when we get into trouble. Without guidance and reassurance to restore comfort positively, I, the dog, will restore comfort levels on my own using behaviors that make sense to me. Those behaviors become "right" to the dog because they work. As long as I'm alive, my response is right, says the dog's mind.

LEARNING FROM THE BEAST

As I wrote earlier in this book, the experience and knowledge I have come from training literally thousands of dogs over the course of my career. But if that's true, then logic will tell you I wasn't always as experienced as I am today. When I think about dogs that have taught me the most about being a trainer, I often think about ones I have owned, because they were the ones I was allowed to work on, even as I was learning the finer points of dog training myself. And, just like any other beginner, I had my share of finding out what doesn't work before I learned what does work.

On the subject of discomfort, I'm reminded of a dog I named Beast. Beast lived in our heated-and-air-conditioned garage, and every day I walked out there to start our morning routine, I let the garage door up. At first, that didn't matter to him, but over time Beast decided the garage door was a discomfort. Through repetition, he associated the garage door going up with a bad thing, and I didn't pick up on that. All I thought about was opening the garage door, letting him out of his crate to go use the bathroom and getting on with the day.

Pretty soon, I started to notice that as I let the garage up, Beast was staring at it. When I went to go open up his kennel, he would shoot past the garage door. It was like he was hesitant, and then he'd shoot past it, and once he was past it while it was open, he's fine. I knew a problem had been created, but I didn't know how to fix it.

Time and experience have helped me see with different eyes. I thought Beast was OK with the garage door because he associated it with me coming out and starting his day. I missed that to him, it was really just a loud, clanking garage door that he'd determined had nothing to do with his survival or comfort. His survival and comfort didn't start, in his mind, until he hit the yard and so all he could think about to deal with the threat was to hurry up and get out of there. He found comfort by escaping it.

Because I didn't correct that discomfort properly—at first because I didn't pick up on it and then because I didn't know what to do about it—I was reinforcing his thought process of once you get past the scary door monster, we're going to come out here and work, doing exercises that we know.

If I had Beast today, the process would be very different from the get-go. As the garage door was going up, I'd go drop food in his kennel and he'd eat it. Once the door was all the way up, I'd pick him up and walk him outside myself. Then, I'd put him on the ground to start the exercise. The message would be that when the garage opens, it's a notification that you're going to get food, which is your survival. And the focus would be more on me and away from the scary door monster because by carrying him out, I eased that discomfort. He didn't have to come up with a solution all by himself. As long as

Calvin was there, Beast was okay.

You don't always learn the best lessons from your successes. Very often, you learn the most important things from your mistakes, and I learned an important one through him.

CHAPTER 3

SURVIVAL

Earlier in this book, I said the two main motivators for a dog are comfort and survival. You can argue that survival is the more powerful of the two because a dog will adapt to uncomfortable situations, but the drive to eat and the drive to protect itself against threats is all-consuming and on the dog's mind daily.

Survival is intertwined with comfort. Survival is that feeling of discomfort over something that might kill you. If your stomach growls, you need to eat. If you're thirsty, you need to drink water. Survival is recognizing what can harm me in any form or fashion. Not eating can harm me, so dogs make associations for eating. They make associations for pain.

In this chapter, we will look at the psychology of survival for your dog, from the effective use of treats and the proper way to feed as a component of training, as well as understanding how the drive to survive shapes the way your dog sees the world. Once you understand these primary drivers, you will be in a much better position to understand how your dog thinks, a critical piece of shaping the animal's behavior.

I WILL SURVIVE

I always marvel at how complicated a dog owner thinks their pet's life is. They try to analyze their beagle like they're Dr. Phil, describing these deep thoughts and motivations that Fluffy has for doing what she does. As I've said many times in this book, this is because people want to diagnose their pets like they are diagnosing another human, and that doesn't work.

People are complicated; dogs are simple. A person's motivations are like a smartphone with multiple settings and functions; a dog's motivations are more like a light switch. I find it funny that people are almost too smart to understand their pet, which thinks on just a couple of levels.

So this is it. This is how a dog operates: Every day, I do what ensures my survival with the least amount of discomfort I can get away with. When the unknown comes along, the unknown is always bad, because I don't know if this thing is going to assist or negatively affect my survival and comfort. Therefore, the unknown is a threat and I have to react accordingly.

As a trainer, my job is to provide experiences that help the animal understand what "react accordingly" means by providing reinforcement and correction in such a way that the dog knows what to do when the unknown approaches. It performs that action because, through repetition, the dog has learned when this happens, I do this, and I get this. That's true in the pack structure, it's true with a skilled trainer, and it is true with a competent dog owner.

Everything that a dog encounters, the dog evaluates to answer one simple, basic question: "Do I like this?" "Like" is usually defined as, "Does it contribute to my survival (like a cheeseburger) or comfort (like jumping up on the couch)." "Don't like" are things that aren't so clear-cut, like a strange noise, a new toy or another animal. In these cases, the dog has to figure out whether to put it in the "like" or "don't like" pile.

As we have seen from the previous chapter, this is not a decision that you want the animal to come up with on their own. For the things they do, like for purposes of survival—such as food—they will do what gets them fed, whether that's hunting a rabbit or sitting on command. For those things they don't like, the goal is to make that thing go away, either through fight or flight.

Keep in mind, "like" and "dislike" look the same in a human's eyes because the puppy is displaying the same behavior in experiencing both options at the moment. Think about a puppy approaching a big dog versus another puppy its size. The puppy's behaviors and demeanor may look very much the same. In fact, it may show barking or puppy-like aggression toward the bigger dog that could obviously harm it. But just because the puppy is showing show-similar behavior doesn't mean that it isn't experiencing likes and dislikes in that particular moment. Very quickly, the puppy learns attraction through association, which informs it whether it likes or dislikes another dog.

Another thing that's really important about the dog's perspective is that Mother Nature fine-tunes some of these survival instincts to innately understand certain threats. Like a lot of animals, dogs don't have to get burned to know to fear fire. Like a lot of animals, dogs don't have to find out the hard way that you don't go sniff a lion just because you're seeing one for the first time. That's because God gave each animal certain instincts that other creatures can pick up. A dog knows not to go and be curious with a lion because a lion gives off the energy that *I'm a preᵈator anᵈ I may kill you.*

There are a lot of people who will tell you they've based their judgment of another person based on their dog's reaction to that person. And there are dogs that are trained to be comfort animals and even "cancer-detecting" animals based on an innate sense of when a person is seriously ill or depressed in some way. Instincts are powerful things.

When a dog decides it doesn't like something, "doesn't like" results in fear, and fear is an uncomfortable emotion. A dog will do whatever it takes to end discomfort, whether that's fight off the thing that's scaring them, run away from the thing that's scaring them, or in the worst case, just surrender to the thing that's scaring them in the sense of showing intimidation and fearful behavior to hope for the best. This last situation is most damaging to the dog's mind, because once they surrender and don't die, they do it every time a new fear presents itself, and the dog lives in fear of everything.

THE POWER OF CHOW

Animals that are domesticated come from wild animals that had to learn how to live in their environment through survival and comfort. Their wild ancestors had to perform behaviors that got them fed to keep living and comfortable in the sense of being out of harm's way. When we learn how to make a dog's meals count and push its comfort levels, it teaches the animal how to live among us.

We can form a super-confident, happy, balanced dog that views life in a similar manner that we do. This makes our dog's life as a companion a whole lot happier because the animal will be able to focus on the relationship with the owner than the scary unknowns that come with this world we live in. There are so many things a dog has to learn on a day-to-day basis, and a regular meal is a great place to start to shape your dog's perception of how to live through its survival and comfort.

On the short list of motivators to survival, the biggest is food. Physical threats generally don't present themselves to the average dog every day; even in the wild, a coyote won't run up on a mountain lion or grizzly bear except every now and then. But every day, a dog gets hungry, and every day the drive to eliminate that hunger (that discomfort) is the top priority.

For the trainer, and the owner after the trainer, food is important on two levels. The one most people think about is using food—specifically treats—to change and reinforce behavior. But something that most dog owners overlook is how critical feeding time is in establishing a relationship with their animal. Let's take a look at both of these uses of food in greater detail.

Think about the daily routine of feeding your dog. Humans are creatures of habit, so it's probably pretty easy to focus on the specific steps you take – what time(s) of day, how much food you provide, what the dog's bowl looks like, the location where feeding takes place, probably even the smell and texture of the food itself.

Every owner is slightly different, but I would imagine the basic process goes something like this: You pick up the bowl, your dog is right there watching your every move, you either scoop the food or open the can, walk to the feeding spot and put down the bowl. Your dog eats and you're done. Right?

This is a process you repeat at least once a day, every day, for the rest of the dog's life. Assuming the lower end of the average lifespan of a dog (10 years or 3,652 days, allowing for two leap years), that's 3,652 repetitions where the dog (and you) did exactly the same thing the same way. (And, if you're wondering, that's more than 7,300 bowls of food if you feed twice a day.)

Now here's an important question: For each of the 3,652

feedings, what did the dog have to do to be fed? If you're like most dog owners, all you required of the dog is that it wakes up and shows up. This is not only a big opportunity wasted every day, it skews the dog's perception. Dogs are hunt animals; way before they were domesticated, they hunted for whatever they ate. In its instinctual self, a dog is still a hunter. Just because the family pet isn't required to chase down and kill what it eats, the dog is wired to take note of which actions it does in order to be fed.

As a trainer, I attach an action to food. This does two things; it reinforces in the dog's mind what to do to get fed, and more importantly, it solidifies in the dog's mind that I am the source of its food and therefore the source of its survival.

So, Square One is teaching the dog how it receives food. I don't put the food down and just walk away. Over a long time frame, if the dog is eating out of the food bowl and I'm nowhere around, the dog is "hunting" by itself for the actual "capture" of the "prey." I don't want to put the dog in a state of mind where it doesn't need me.

I feed dogs by hand for this very reason, and it's a practice not everybody agrees with. People think the dog won't get enough food that way or that they have to be super-hungry to eat food out of your hand. This simply isn't true; the average dog eats (or should eat) just three cups of food per day, an amount I can easily dispense by hand as a reward for doing its work throughout the day. That leaves no doubt in the dog's mind that it is dependent on me for its food and, therefore, its survival.

A nice byproduct of feeding by hand is you're less likely to overfeed a dog than you are just by filling up a bowl. Just like people, dogs will overeat just because there's food in front of them. If you've seen an overweight dog, it's not overweight because it requires more food than normal or that it is hungrier than the average dog. The dog overeats because it's become a conditioned behavior to do so. Just like you can teach a dog to sit, you can teach a dog to overeat.

On the other hand, a dog that you feed regularly with your hand will eventually refuse food if it's not hungry because the natural state of mind tells the dog that when it is full, its effort should stop. That makes it less likely the dog will overeat and be overweight, which, in turn, avoids a whole host of costly health problems.

So, getting the dog to understand food comes from you is a big plus when it comes to training and reinforcing behavior. It's also relationship building. Remember when we said the dog has to trust you on some level in order to follow your commands? There's no stronger trust bond for a dog than to consider you the source of its survival.

FOOD AS A TRAINING TOOL

Once you've gotten over the urge to fill up a bowl and feed the dog by hand, you can start to understand how to use food/treats during the actual training process. I tell people to have all types of treats at their house, so once the dog makes the association with their dog food and has had its fill of food, the treat is smelly enough to give them something as a reward to whatever behavior you're seeing.

The next step would be to actually keep the food on your person, meaning in a pocket or a jacket. Get the same amount and pull it from your pocket or jacket so that the dog will start to look at you like a vending machine. You don't necessarily know what's in the vending machine until you perform an action of good behavior. Demonstrating those behaviors is like putting quarters in the vending machine, pressing the button, and the reward has dispensed. Eventually, the dog starts to look at you like, "Hey, vending machine, what do I do?"

Once you get that dog's attention and once that dog starts looking forward to you, you control that part of the animal's life and you can start capitalizing off of offered behaviors that result in the dog performing a sit, wait or down. That's what you call *free shaping*; it may do something, and once it does that something, you pull out food and dispense it. It's really to what extent the dog values something that will dictate what you can convince it to do in terms of behavior.

It's important to know that this kind of reinforcement happens all the time, whether you are intentional about it or not. For instance, many dog owners hand out treats "just because" or to "show the animal they love them." Well, dogs don't see it the way you intend it; they make a note of what they are doing at the time and resolve to do that every time they have room for food.

So, if a dog is barking and barking, and you just give it a treat— *Voila!* You just taught that dog that barking equals food. Since barking was the dog's idea, the dog can tap into that idea a lot faster. It's going to revert back to that state of mind all of the time because it thought of that thing by itself. It pushed your buttons and made you do something. You reinforced it with a high-value reward.

Don't give your dog food just to give them food; that's the perfect opportunity to train them. Let's say you fill a dog up on unnecessary amounts of food, then take it outside potty, a car drives by and it gets scared. To the dog's mind, in survival and comfort, that car might have made him uncomfortable and most definitely could dictate his survival. "It's loud, it startled me, and it might come to kill me." Normally, that's the perfect time to reinforce calm behavior with a treat, but you can't because the dog is already full and food doesn't have high value as when it is hungry.

Now compare that to a dog who isn't stuffed and full and is looking forward to going outside to potty. The car comes by, I can reinforce with food the moment the dog askes himself, "What is that?" and I can immediately answer that with "It's a positive" by paring it to the food.

Food is a powerful connector, whether it's your family around the Thanksgiving dinner table or one-on-one with your dog. You've heard the definition of the Golden Rule: "He who has the gold makes the rules." Well, in the dog world, it's more like, "He who has the treats calls the shots."

DITCH THE DISH

For those who are adopting an adult dog from a shelter, first of all, great. Too many really good animals die in shelters every year because people go right for the puppies, or they go through other sources before looking at the local animal shelter. Every day, dogs are euthanized in shelters because workers or potential owners don't possess the knowledge to retrain their brain or know the amount of time it would take. If this was known, a majority of these dogs could be saved.

Shelters really do some great work, but because there are so many animals to care for, very few of them have the manpower to feed hundreds of dogs from the hand or attach food to a specific behavior. So, they fill the bowl and move on, and most owners continue this action day after day.

Many shelter dogs come from situations where they have had to fend for themselves in the street or dig through garbage or whatever to get their meals. Almost every bite of food they ever got came from their ability to figure out how to get it. So, it stands to logic that it will take some work for a dog like that to eat from the hand and learn to rely on the human as the source for their food and not just their own wits.

Either way, if a dog comes from the shelter, it needs to be fed out of your hand. This might seem a little iffy as you're getting used to each other and the animal is learning to trust you. You can start by holding a food bowl and letting them eat from that at first. Whatever it takes, you want to establish that food comes from you and not from the dog's own ingenuity.

Early on in the process, don't attach food to an action or command. Your goal here is just getting that dog used to being able to receive food from the hand without any exercises and no commands. It's simple; you have the food in a bag or on your person, and you only take out the amount you want the dog to eat at that moment. And even though the food bag is here, I'm not going to let you jump on it and tear the bag open. I dispense it, it's coming from me, every time. This is the first step to everything else you want the dog to do.[1]

---

1 Ditching the dish doesn't mean you will forever feed your dog out of your hand. we have to realize that the dog sees it's food bowl as a jackpot so once you've mastered being it's source you will be able to give the dog its food bowl after it's earned.

CHAPTER 4

EAT OR BE EATEN

When I was young, about 13 or 14, I witnessed five-week-old puppies being afraid of me. It brought out curiosity in me: How do these little puppies know whether or not I'm dangerous?

You can probably guess it by now: Survival and comfort!

I've had nothing to do with their survival and I've never comforted them. Therefore, seeing me for the first time, they don't automatically think of me as something positive. In fact, they see it as their survival may be at stake if they come to me or if I get too close.

Earlier in this book, I shared the example I use all the time with clients about dogs and aliens. Humans are like aliens to the dog. Even if they do get used to you, there are still other aliens out there walking around. Now, dogs know that even though they were afraid of aliens (humans), this particular alien (you) showed me (the dog) time after time that he's not a bad alien. The dog will look at you as an individual and maybe the exception. Everyone else is still an alien who is, in their mind, still able to hurt or kill them. But this is not how we want them to think. When I bring in a dog that may have these problems, my job isn't to make a dog think it's my dog but rather to make the dog understand what its relationship is to humans.

My goal as a trainer is to produce a dog that isn't afraid of anything. I keep bringing up fear because I've seen way too many decent, confident dogs that have something that bothers them. The dog can get scared of something so quickly, things the owner doesn't catch. Dogs often display fear in ways we don't notice, such as cowering, ears down and tail between the legs. Sometimes fear is expressed as aggression, and so that also confuses things. A client comes to me with a dog and says, "He's overly aggressive," when in fact, it's just the way the dog is dealing with fear.

This chapter will deal with getting at the real issues with your dog instead of just looking at its behavior. I'll also talk about ways I deal with the most common issues dogs have in a world where, to their understanding, it's always "eat or be eaten."

THE WORLD'S A SCARY PLACE

A dog's behavior can tell you a lot, but it gets misinterpreted by owners all the time. They'll say that's their confident dog. In all honesty, a water gun can scare them, and now you're wondering why it's super afraid of the water gun. On the other hand, I've seen a dog that was wagging its tail and playing with you and then all of a sudden wants to bite you in the face. Most dogs are in the shelter because people don't understand the fine line between how dogs become good and how dogs become bad.

As I said before, when you're considering owning a dog, it's very important to check the backstory of the dog. Sometimes that's easier said than done. For lots of dogs in the shelter, the majority, in fact, we only have limited information. If the dog was rescued from a bad situation, you could make a pretty good guess about what the dog has been through, but it's probably impossible to get any more specific than that.

Rescue organizations, on the other hand, are sometimes different because these groups often use foster families to house the dog until it is adopted. Foster families deal with the dog on a day-in, day-out basis and can provide more details on how the dog acts around people, other pets, kids and different situations. Again, it doesn't tell you everything, but it might give you more information to work with.

Regardless, I would always recommend consulting a professional that's done a lot of behavioral training to provide training for their dog. Dog owners need to accept that training their dog is going to be a process. It's a process within a process because between the ages of three to three and a half years old, that behavior was so consistent that that's all the dog knows. No matter what situation a dog was in, if it survived and found food by being scared or aggressive or whatever, that's what works, and that's what is set in the animal's mind as the way to behave to ensure survival and comfort.

Here's the good news: sound training is effective an overwhelming percentage of the time. I don't care how good a dog is, how sad a dog is, how stubborn or whatever; unless the dog has some kind of mental defect, every dog has the ability to adapt and change. That's part of their nature. Anyone serious about adopting a dog needs to be serious in accepting what goes along with it and how long the timeframe could be to retrain its thought process and behavior.

STOP, HEY, WHAT'S THAT SOUND?

Dogs are amazing, powerful creatures, yet I have seen dogs that would scare you to see them act like crybabies over the strangest things. What makes a giant German shepherd or a bowed-up pitbull whimper over the ice maker in the fridge?

A dog that's fearful thinks demonstrating scared behavior helps it stay alive. In their mind, if something happened that scared them and they came out of it in one piece, then whatever reaction the dog had is perceived as the reason why. Dog logic: *The noisy truck drove by. I couldn't run, I couldn't attack it, but I lived anyway. Well, what did I do? I know! I felt scared, and that's apparently the key to surviving that uncomfortable situation. I'll go with that from now on.*

Dog's don't understand that being calm and ignoring the "threat" would have worked just as well. The emotion of being startled or flinching, which happens as a reflex, is what they felt first. Without training to the contrary, they'll continue to rely on that as the behavior that will allow them to live to see tomorrow, and you get a dog that is progressively more fearful. All the more reason to understand and take control of the associations.

As we've said before, you don't want your dog to make up their own mind on how to deal with discomfort and fear. A fearful dog got that way because at the time it got scared of something, there was no one there to ease its discomfort; no one it could trust to give the energy and reinforcement that there was nothing to be scared of and instill in the dog a mindset where the scary thing became a "familiar alien." The dog still doesn't know what that thing is, but it's been conditioned that the thing won't affect its survival or comfort, so the dog ignores it.

Remember, dogs don't have a third category to put things in; it's always about the impact of survival and comfort.

Let's say you're walking with a puppy and they see somebody in the distance for the first time. They say, "What's that?"

If you don't do anything, they say, "Is it coming at me?" That's another mindset.

Then, they say, "What could he possibly do to me?"

Then, "He may kill me."

Then, "Well, I never needed him."

Then, "Oh my God, it is getting closer!"

In those steps that I just listed, I don't let a dog's mindset escalate past "What is that?" By using the clicker, *"Click! Click! Click!"* has now turned their curiosity into a positive and then they get food from me.

Now, through repetition, as soon as they look, I change their state of mind to positive. When you look at that, you need it because it's going to get you food. Now, the puppy looks at you, at it, and then back at you. In their mind, it's clear.

I use the same basic formula when I intentionally introduce dogs to unfamiliar places, such as a busy shopping center or a big sporting goods store. I'm watching the dog very closely, and every time it starts demonstrating that "What's that?" look and posture, I reinforce the good mindset until, eventually, the dog learns that whatever it sees or hears, the only thing that matters is me, the source of its comfort and survival. If Calvin says it's cool, then it's cool.

Let's say you had to take a long trip with your dog that not only required being in a busy, unfamiliar place, but made it have to accept things that he normally wouldn't get near. When I took Primo on a trip to California, he'd never been in an airport, on an escalator, or on an airplane before. But because I have him conditioned to know that I am always thinking about his health and welfare, none of that bothered him. He'd check at times, like, "Hey, man, what do we think of this?" But as long as I didn't respond to it, neither did he.

Now, that's not an entirely fair example, because of how much time and training Primo has had. So, let's take that same scenario, take him out of it and insert a puppy. The puppy sees the escalator. They see it's moving. They look at it—*Click! Click! Click!* You step backwards, get his attention off of the escalator, and he gets food. Remember when I said your dog should see you as their vending machine? Well, the escalator is now a quarter he just found to make the vending machine give it a snack. They start making these associations that, when I look at it, it produces something. They've stopped thinking that it's scary; they know it's good, and you have been the determining factor to what is good.

Now, I take the puppy, I get them closer to the escalator and, once I realize that they're focused on me and they're leaning forward trying to sniff it before they get on it, and show that they know for a fact that the click is going to happen, that's when we get on. I'll give them some high-value food like some chicken breast to reinforce and maintain that feeling.

Once we get off of it, I put the puppy down. *Click! Click! Click!* I give the puppy food and I just move on. I want the puppy to think, "Wow, we just got done with that and that's how I got my food. I want to go back to it, but, since we're moving forward, I'm fine with that. I want to continue on."

To the dog, the clicker is like a notification on your phone, reminding you to do something or making you feel a certain way when you get a text message from your significant other. And it works with anything new or unfamiliar when you see the dog is demonstrating "What's that?" posture or behavior. If you see that a dog is afraid of people, for instance, and they look at a person, you *Click! Click! Click!* and give them food. Over time, you'll turn their mindset from being fearful and going beyond "What's that?" to deeper thoughts in their mind.

DEALING WITH AGGRESSION

Dogs are aggressive for a number of reasons—they may have been taught to be aggressive as in the case of a dog raised to fight; they may be overstepping their bounds to get control of the pack, or it may be a response to fear and a feeling of being cornered.

Certain breeds have the reputation of naturally being more aggressive than others. That's not the case. I have taken pitbulls bred for fighting and turned them into great family dogs, and I have seen chihuahuas dominate bigger dogs within a household. While it is true that some breeds do have attributes that lend themselves to work that calls for strength and aggression—like a German shepherd for protection—aggression levels ARE NOT an automatic with any breed.

There are a lot of factors tied to dog aggression, and there are different levels to see if a dog is aggressive. Let's say if you're driving a car and your dog sees a dog. Once you pass, how long does it take to forget about the dog? Was it a, *"Hey! There's a dog!"* with a little whimper, and then we're on the road? Or was it a running to the back of the car, whimpering, whining and really wanting to get out? How does that dog look when it encounters another dog? If you put another dog nearby in a crate, will he stick around and try to tear that crate open to get at it? Is the dog uneasy around dogs?

In some cases, the dog is too far gone to be retrained, but that is rare. If the dog is in a situation where it's aggressive towards people, there are specific exercises a qualified and experienced trainer can do that can help, even if the dog is three or four years old.

My personal dog, Primo, had dog aggression. I hated it. I absolutely hated it. But I didn't deal with dog aggression by taking him around other dogs and socializing. We got him at five months and he was really dog-aggressive. For the first three or four months, I was just teaching him who I was. Once a dog can trust me and know everything comes from me, then I can start to introduce him to things.

When it comes time to introduce other dogs to him, it's not necessarily him going to play at a dog park. It's not about that. It's about him being around a dog while still being focused on me. He can take in what the environment has to offer. We consider that background noise. If my dog has positive experiences being around other dogs, he knows that they aren't a threat; therefore, he can always focus on me even with the other distractions. A dog has instincts.

At the end of the day, you're just trying to get your dog to collect the energy from another dog without being super-focused on that other dog. That energy, if not focused on you, can be taken as a threat, and this is what happens when people allow their dogs to make decisions on their own when it comes to other dogs.

With kids, it's better to teach the dog how to withstand everything. My dog used to be very fearful. But through learning his survival and comfort, I can introduce him to almost anything and he'll adopt it as if it was his own. Now, my son's presence doesn't bother him—well, actually, my son bothers him a lot—but mentally, my dog isn't affected. He understands that I'm allowing something to happen. He shouldn't have to fend for himself.

I've taught dogs that were supposed to go into homes to withstand anything. A dog can actually associate pain with a good thing. That's another way dogs don't think like people. What that means is that I teach puppies by starting off light; you barely apply pressure to their foot, and you feed. I grab their tails. I grab their skin. I grab their ears, and I feed. I grab their muzzle, and I feed. Now, of course, each dog is different. If you come across too firm, the puppy will have a reaction. But, doing it in a way where the puppy doesn't show any reaction gets it used to those touches through repetition. Then you can up the ante on physical touch to where it can withstand more.

If the dog understands who the person is and they understand this person's relationship, they should trust that the person isn't going to put them in any situation where they're going to be fearful. That goes for the trainer, and that goes for the owner, once the dog gets home and the kids are crawling all over the animal to play with it. It's all about the dog's associations.

START 'EM EARLY

Confident puppies or pups that seem to not have any problems can basically grow up to become hyper-sensitive to touch, and this can be on any area of their body. Think about cases where dogs have bitten a child or an adult; in the dog's mind, it's not being aggressive. Improper or lack of training causes the dog to believe that it has to react in that way to find comfort. It's using the only option it thinks it has to ease its discomfort. Bottom line: a dog finds itself uncomfortable in a situation where a person (especially a kid) grabs or either touches them the wrong way.

A dog that's been going through life with minor uncomfortable situations and has been allowed to escape them with moderate growling, or that simply escapes the area or presence of a perceived threatening person, will one day find itself in a situation where there's no such escape. The "threat" doesn't go away when the dog growls at it. The animal is "cornered" and can't run. The result, naturally, is a bite.

This is, obviously, a bad outcome on its own, but it goes deeper. When that same dog experiences that level of serious discomfort, the animal remembers it vividly, sometimes over the course of years. A situation, that may have only presented itself a few times to the dog, is set in its mind to where each incident sends a strong signal to the animal's brain. The dog knows in his soul he hates "Discomfort X."

As a trainer, I highly recommend forming associations through intentional conditioning that demonstrates to the dog how it can exert its options of escaping discomfort in a way that's positive, and that over-reacting to the situation (biting, peeing, etc.) doesn't work. Remember, show a dog that something it's doing doesn't work, and they will abandon that as an option.

Let's use the example of a puppy wanting to escape the discomfort of being touched or held, what the dog perceives as a category of "pain." As usual, I am not talking about what you and I would consider intense, serious pain here, but what the dog thinks. Imagine the last puppy you owned that your child tried to play with; chances are, at some point in the moment of picking a pup up, it was uncomfortable, and it likely started to whine/growl and even try to bite. Obviously, the puppy isn't being hurt, it's just experiencing discomfort, so we have to teach the dog that the touches aren't bad things.

Here's what I do: I make associations with the lightest grabs on the ears, tail, legs and the side of the puppy's belly. Early on, food is released into the puppy's mouth as I grab an area on their body, then I progress to releasing food after I've grabbed them. The dog is learning that everything about its survival comes from me and is thinking, "Calvin tugged on my ears, I lived AND I got a reward, so this must be OK."

If the puppy demonstrates discomfort over being picked up, don't just put the pup down right away. If you do that, you are teaching the animal that freaking out brings it comfort instead of being calm. I hold the pup in that position until it runs out of options (whine, squirm, try to bite, etc.) and it just goes calm. Through repetition and consistency, the dog learns that being slightly uncomfortable is an OK thing.

BELLA

Bella is a client's dog who was brought to me with extreme fear. She's a good example of how fear can be misdiagnosed in a dog and left to get progressively worse with each passing day.

Bella is a dog that's super afraid of a person walking towards her and everything else, for that matter. She's got this look in her eyes like she's convinced that everything in the world is about to kill her. Most people, who saw a dog with the issues that Bella had, would assume that she had been mistreated. Nothing could be further from the truth. I told the owner, "I'm pretty sure you gave this dog the world, but she doesn't view it like that."

People think because they give their dog a great lifestyle, that they're setting them up to be happy and well-adjusted. In all honesty, you can make the worst dog possible, because you're so sure you're doing right by the dog that you don't look for what they perceive as wrong. A dog may live in the biggest home ever. Dogs don't care about that. They could have every toy and their own room with air conditioning, and the dog would not care. All they care about is comfort and survival and how they deal with the unknown, which, as you know by now, is always seen as a threat. Remember: "unknown" equals "don't like" and "don't like" equals "fear."

Bella was raised with other dogs, and she took so many cues from them that she basically never learned how to deal with life on her own. The owner didn't understand that it was their role to help her make the right associations, and since they didn't do that, she was always fearful and stressed out. In extreme cases, I've seen dogs die from being so stressed out over not being able to cope.

With Bella, the associations were off once you took the other dogs out of the equation. Bella was howling every night, looking for her pack. It's the only way she knew to survive. The owner didn't understand that her associations were off and what a dog learns when they don't make the right associations. It's allowed to be afraid, and the owner is a part of that.

The challenge for me was to reprogram her mind and say, "OK, now the key to survival is through the human. It's not through other dogs." Even though I am a different species, that's the dominion we have over dogs. We're able to take them, mold and shape them based on their beliefs, comfort and survival. I have to tell you, I've been in this game a long time, and I've never had a challenge quite like her. She began to stress me out with how she viewed things mentally. It was actually sad; it was almost like dealing with a dog with multiple personalities.

I can look at a dog and know that it's never been hit a day in its life, but to the rest of the world, that's not what they see. Bella was afraid of me; every time I went to go and touch her, she'd take off running. If she ever was to get loose, she would make it all the way down to the next city.

One of my assistant trainers said to me, "I wonder if she's ever been beaten before?"

I said, "I'm 100 percent sure that this dog hasn't even had a rough touch at all."

So, here's the point: People should know that fear in the dog can be presented in the same way, whether that dog has been beaten or not, due to associations. I was able to solve Bella's problems by addressing and acknowledging her survival and comfort instincts.

CHAPTER 5

THE ENERGY OF OTHERS

We've said several times in this book that the last thing you want a dog to do is to figure out how to deal with a situation or determine appropriate behavior for themselves. Right next to that is being influenced by other dogs, which is always a consideration in a household where there are multiple animals.

Up to now, all we've talked about is how to bring your dog's understanding in line with what you want it to do and how you want it to behave. In other words, the appropriate way for the dog to live in your house and your world. When we start talking about the pack mentality, we're flipping the script a little bit, because we're now looking at how you must function effectively in the dog's natural view of life—the laws of the pack.

In this chapter, we'll talk about the law of the pack, how it rules a dog's thinking even when it's the only animal in a home, how to claim your place at the head of the pack as the dog owner and how to manage the pack mentality effectively.

LEADER OF THE PACK

When it comes to people and their dogs, pack mentality is very important in matters of socialization and environment. No amount of training, domestication or time has ever eliminated the pack mentality from a dog. It's just who and what they are, handed down across millions of years of evolution and instinct. That's why it's so important that every dog owner understands what it is and how it works.

There is not a situation involving a dog where the pack mentality does not apply. Dogs see each other the way that they see everything: through instincts, through their vibe, with their energy. A dog can tell that another dog is a dog because of the energy it produces, compared to a rabbit or a lion or whatever other animal you want to name.

Within the pack, there's an alpha. The alpha sets the tone, gives the orders, calls the shots. Within a mixed pack, there's an alpha male and alpha female, but there's only one clear leader. The female has been known to take a back seat to the male in these situations, but not always. All members of the pack know and submit to the power of the alpha as a leader.

Alpha status instinctually gives the dog special privileges, and this is how you can tell which of your dogs is asserting dominance. For instance, if you feed them all at the same time, the alpha will more than likely be the dog that can limit others from feeding. This can result in the alpha biting or nipping the others as a signal to stop eating.

Don't assume the bigger or older of two dogs is automatically the alpha. While these traits often give one dog an advantage over the other, alpha status is as much mental as it is physical. I've been to a client's house where a Jack Russell Terrier dominated a group of German shepherds.

Dogs don't see size. It's about the energy that is being put out. For example, size matters and comes into effect when you have a super-confident little dog that's bullying a bigger dog and the bigger dog realizes that he has to protect himself. It will explode on the smaller dog. Until that happens, a Jack Russell Terrier with the confidence to go after the German shepherds is thinking, "This is me. I'm head honcho."

The owner has to pay very close attention to what's going on, because whether you know it or not, you're part of the pack, too. Dogs will adopt you if you allow them. They're not supposed to adopt you; you're supposed to adopt them. Let's say they adopt you into the pack and something freakish were to happen. They will correct you with a bite or another physical gesture.

The way that your dog views you is very important. Either you're in the pack, or you run the pack. If you let a dog fight another dog, they will challenge you one day. I've seen people who are within the pack get hurt by their dogs. They say, "I don't get it. This dog's been nice the whole time." Well, his behavior was on point with what they thought was a nice dog, but when the dog feels like the owner did something wrong, the dog will decide to correct them!

Think of it this way: Your mom loves you and is a gentle person until you need correcting; then, she's swatting your behind. You might not like it, but you're not surprised by her authority to spank you because you know she outranks you in the family structure.

The pack functions in much the same way. If you allow any dog to take control over the pack situations, then you're allowing them to create their status. You can lose control of your household really quickly. I'll never let that happen, but a lot of dog owners do, and, not surprisingly, the dog begins to dominate the owner.

We have dominion over animals, not just certain breeds, and so my primary role as the alpha in my pack is to keep order. I make sure I dictate behaviors, stopping some and encouraging others. I shape that dog's lifestyle based on the knowledge I have about the dog itself.

I've seen a pack of poodles with a tiny chihuahua that runs everything. It scares the dogs off and won't let them eat. I'm never OK with a dog showing this type of dominance. No matter how many times they try that, I interfere, and that begins to shape how the dogs view me for life.

At the end of the day, I'm the one who feeds them, and the dogs start to learn that their survival comes through me. By controlling these things that the dog needs, the dog will start to look at you like, "This is Alpha!"

Me being alpha in my packs has also helped me really understand that all dogs are essentially the same. Some dogs have different traits that they were bred for. But, when it comes to the mind of a dog and how they deal with humans and other animals, there's very little that's different. Whether it's a German Shepherd, Malamute, Pitbull, Poodle, Rottweiler, Shih Tzu, Chihuahua, Great Dane or Bull Mastiff, it all comes down to having the instinct of dealing with a person by how they view a person.

THE PACK AND TRAINING

Establishing and maintaining the role of the alpha is critically important to training dogs. It's particularly challenging for people who have multiple dogs to keep the true say-so in a relationship, not allowing dogs to fight, not allowing them to run over you, chew on things, how you feed them. That's the dominion part.

I don't allow dogs to be around each other 24/7. If anything, their time with each other is limited, and when I do work them, I work them separately. My advice for people thinking about getting multiple dogs is to create a schedule for working with one dog and then, once that dog understands its lifestyle, bring another dog into the fold. Only get a second dog after you know your first dog is going to handle business the way you want inside of the house.

There are little things that dog owners do that make their life harder and create more problems for them. Dropping your dog off to a family member and then leaving for a while is probably not the smartest thing, unless that family member is willing to give 100 percent to make sure that dog's life is in keeping with the same life that you left it with.

When training a dog, I would be sure you're confident in your dog's socialization skills before sending them to doggie daycare. Additionally, you want to be careful about the boarding facilities you choose when you have to go out of town. At my facility, we do board dogs, but since we are trainers first, there's no disconnect between what you're trying to do at home and what we do here.

In the beginning stages of a dog's life, multiple dogs should not be left together when dog owners leave for work or to run errands for an extended amount of time. They can be by themselves, but not together. Use the crate to keep them apart when you're not there to monitor and reinforce correct behavior. On this same token, I don't let puppies just meet and play with other puppies, either.

You may think separating dogs like this results in socialization issues, but I've got thousands of examples to the contrary. In fact, I have dogs that are so extremely social with other people and extremely social with other dogs that people often ask, "Did you let him be around other dogs? You put him around *goo* dogs, didn't you?"

What they don't know is, just like anything else in the dog's life, I'm allowing socialization with a purpose. I'm not just turning dogs loose together and letting them figure things out on their own. A big mistake people make with their dogs is that they tend to let dogs do whatever they want to do. You're just asking for problems when you do this.

If you can't work with a puppy and you know that the environment isn't consistent, and if the puppy is too curious, put it in the crate until you can give it 100 percent of your effort. That not only keeps the puppy from being influenced by other dogs, but it takes away environmental influences. Putting the dog in its crate also teaches it how to be independent. That's a very important factor. You want your dog to learn independence.

A LESSON IN DOMINANCE

Everything I put in this book is a result of years of dog training, during which time I have handled and worked with dogs of many different breeds and backgrounds. I've been bitten and scratched many times, knocked down, made mistakes. Each time I came back wiser and more determined than I was before.

I owe my start in this business to a man named Cecil Brannon. I first met Cecil when I wandered over to his dog training facility as a 13-year-old boy. I knew then I wanted to train dogs, but he couldn't see that, and he figured I was just another kid who would turn my attention to something else before long. A few years went by, and I started showing up at his Saturday training sessions. I wasn't even getting paid, but I was always there. I was that hungry to get involved in training and learn everything I could.

Cecil had funny ways of motivating people. He joked around a lot. I'd do something crazy or misread a dog, and he would make me feel like what I lacked was common sense. I loved training so much that my mind started to work in a way like, *"I'm going to make sure this guy A) Can't get ma• at me, an• B) Can't make fun of me."*

One day, Cecil threw me in a bite suit for the first time and handed me the biggest, "baddest" dog I've ever had in my life. This dog was named Jazz. Jazz was a German shepherd that weighed about 125 pounds. Yeah!

The reason I put the suit on, outside of curiosity, was because I never told authority no. But I tell you, I was really conflicted. A part of me was scared, and a part of me was like, "Do it."

So, I jumped in the suit, and I was like, "What do I do?"

Cecil said, "Just put your arms in the suit and take off running."

I said, "What do I do then?"

He was like, "The dog will do the rest."

I was so scared; I was running, and all I can remember was looking back. The dog hadn't been released yet. Cecil was letting me get a long way away from this dog, and I'm thinking in my mind, "The farther I get, the faster he's going to get."

I heard steps like a horse. When I was about to turn my head, this dog bit me in my back and lifted me up. He was toting me and had literally picked me up off the ground for more than five yards before I fell. I remember seeing the blue sky, and I remember people laughing. I kept hearing, "Get up! Get up!" Every time I'd try to get up, this dog would snatch me to the ground.

When I finally got up, my body was just shocked. I was like, what happened? I just got attacked by an animal. Long story short, I said that would never happen again. Cecil triggered a lot of things in me, most of all to be extremely focused on trying to become somebody. It just put a fire in me that, I promise you, has never left through my whole career.

CHAPTER 6

LIKES AND DISLIKES

Most of the topics I have covered so far in this book have been dealt with in absolutes. All dogs are influenced by the pack mentality, and all dogs are focused on comfort and survival. That's not to say that all dogs are created equal, learn at the same rate, or see things exactly the same way. If that were true, then anyone could train a dog, just by making all their mistakes with the first one and then getting another one.

The fact of the matter is, dogs have personalities and learning styles just like people do. And some dogs are more engaged in the process of training than others. Just like people, there are dogs who are energetic and enthusiastic about their learning, and there are those who aren't. The problem with this is, dog owners tend to give the dog too much credit for what it "likes" and what it "dislikes" or finds "uncomfortable."

It's way too easy to let this perception of your dog give it more of a say-so in how things run at your house than it's entitled to. Dogs develop behaviors because we allow the dog to access a state of mind where it processed a situation and downloaded behavior. We capture the feelings the dog had toward something before they can process it as bad and quickly turn it into a positive.

Much of this comes down to observation and a willingness by the owner to not bend the rules. I get a lot of clients who talk about a dog's "favorite" this or that. Some people will tell you to tuck a new puppy into its crate with the owner's t-shirt or some other items that carry their scent, which is supposed to more quickly socialize the dog.

Personally, I don't consider that effective, and, in a way, it lets the owner off the hook of doing what they are supposed to do to help train or maintain their dog's learned skills. You're asking the t-shirt to teach the dog how to react when the clothes dryer kicks on or when they see something that looks unfamiliar and makes them uneasy. That's your job!!!

Another reason that doesn't work is that dogs aren't sentimental or nostalgic; they don't get a better feeling from a brand-new toy than they do with a toy they've had for years. Their brains don't work that way. Let's say, for instance, you switch your dog's food from a brand it's eaten all along, then switch back—do you think you'd see any difference in the dog's excitement to eat? No, because it's the eating, not the brand name of the food that matters to a dog.

Ideally, a dog should have no habits, likes or preferences apart from what you've taught it, intentionally or unintentionally, through reinforcement. That doesn't mean as a trainer that I'm creating a robot. Even my most highly skilled dog screws up or starts to test me. A certain amount of that is to be expected, but an owner who caves into it is creating real problems. I see it all the time. And it goes back to what we said in the opening pages of this book about relating to your dog as if it thought like a human.

For example, people think that military dogs, law enforcement dogs and personal protection dogs (and to a lesser extent, hunting dogs) are somehow special because they willingly go into harm's way at the command of their handler. A bomb-sniffing dog is no more what we'd call "brave" or self-sacrificing than a mutt out in the yard. It's just been highly trained to perform a certain sequence of tasks to receive reinforcement. And, the dog doesn't do it just to be a good boy or for self-esteem or satisfaction of saving a life. People do things for the sake of doing them; dogs do it to survive and stay comfortable.

It's very hard for people to understand this concept, because they don't take it from the dog's perspective. Take personal protection training, for instance. What you want is a dog that keeps coming forward even after it's been hit, even though it would "prefer" to just run off out of harm's way and be done with it. If you think a dog will stand there and fight for you to the death because it "loves" you, think again. Dogs are selfish creatures; training overrides a natural response (fleeing) by teaching an unnatural action (advancing).

Well, the nature of the task requires a certain type of training. That dog is going to get hit one day protecting its owner – it just comes with the territory. Without proper training, the dog will run away from the attacker that hits it, because running away protects its survival, and it's more comfortable than fighting and risking getting hit again. Here again, people outside of the dog training world don't understand what it takes to make that happen.

I teach a dog through repetition of me pushing it back, and when it comes forward, it gets food. Then, I started adding a little pop with my hand versus a little push. Then I start pushing off with my leg, and when the dog comes back forward, it gets food. By the time I near the end of training with a dog, I'll be able to give him merely a rough little push with my leg to activate it.

Now, you might be asking, if the dog is seeking comfort, why does an uncomfortable action work? The way that people view pain for humans isn't the same way with dogs and how they view it. It's not natural for people to get struck. But for a dog, it doesn't matter. They're just trying to seek survival and comfort. So now, when Mr. Bad Guy tries to fight the dog off by hitting it, it triggers the "advance" instinct because that's what the dog knows will get it a reward.

Let's consider a competition dog, where it has to perform these complicated maneuvers that are very unnatural to the average dog. To the trained animal, it's not unnatural at all as long as the owner is consistent and never leads the dog into a situation where its survival and comfort are threatened.

People who don't understand this or can't understand their dog's mindset make all kinds of mistakes. Number one is, they let a dog start to get away with things. Let's say you're trying to teach your dog to sit and stay. Fluffy gets "sit" right, but when you walk off, the dog is on its feet and following you. What do you do? A bad dog owner will try a couple more times and then generally give up and give a treat for getting the "sit" part right. Well, what have you really told that dog? That it's OK to selectively obey, to follow certain commands and ignore other ones. It's like shaking the vending machine to steal a treat versus dropping in a coin and buying one.

Here's another situation: Let's say you're committed to practice sit-stay all weekend if you have to. The dog gets up and starts walking instead of staying put. You say "sit" again, which the dog does. Well, unless you walked the dog back to its original spot to start over, you've reinforced to the dog that it's still OK not to obey, as long as I keep it within a few steps in the direction where I wanted to go. It might seem like a small thing, but it plants a seed to the dog that they have some say in what you want it to do.

You can take this in a lot of different directions when you are training or trying to reinforce your trainer's work. For instance, how many times you give a command. Give your dog the "down" command more than once, and it'll know that every time it gets a command, it's like the first bell back in high school. Now your dog is thinking, "I'm not really in trouble until the second bell rings, so the first one is just kind of a warm-up." And, if you give the dog a treat because it did the action (after multiple commands), all you do is reinforce that "second bell" mentality.

I cannot say it loudly or strongly enough: You are always training your dog, whether you mean to or not.

The laxer you allow the dog to be in following commands just makes the animal wonder how far they can push things and still get comfort and survival. This is the only time you will hear me say that your dog, in theory, is just like your child. What you need to understand is when you start cutting corners, it's not going to do anything but grow. If little Timmy didn't get a cupcake right away as a toddler, but you gave it to him just because he cried, when he's 17, he'll have a tantrum and give you attitude because you didn't respond to him fast enough. You created that behavior by allowing it to happen.

The bottom line is this: Changing behavior is always uncomfortable, but through discomfort, the dog can improve and adapt. If a puppy doesn't want to go for a walk, scoot it with your foot until it complies. If your dog scratches at the kennel to get out when you want it in there, leave the puppy alone. It will stop when it's been unsuccessful at getting out.

Rewarding half-compliance makes it the new full-compliance in the dog's mind. Anything on this earth, through repetition, becomes more ingrained in our memory. Remember, you are in control of your dog's likes and dislikes until you're not.

TAKING THE SHOW ON THE ROAD

I sold a dog to a client, and that client felt he should be able to take that dog anywhere and everywhere, and it would perform to his standards. If that dog does not meet the owner's expectations, the dog should be trained more. On one level, the client was absolutely right to think that. But, on another level, his perspective was wrong.

If I get a puppy and take it to Walmart, the park, or somewhere else where it is around other dogs, other people or both, the dog is learning more reasons to not trust me because of all the things that are going on and bothering that dog. The proper thing, no matter a puppy or an adult animal, is to form a routine and a relationship with that dog first and then take that dog places. Use your same routine and consistency when you travel or go out in public.

When a dog doesn't have a routine and you decide to take that dog out, it will not display the level of obedience you're expecting. Dogs are able to transition to different environments and make associations with anything that dictates their comfort. If I had anything to do with that dog's comfort and survival and then passed it off to you, of course, I now have to teach you to manipulate and maintain this dog's comfort and survival.

What's going to happen through repetition is you're going to take this dog places, and it's going to be uncomfortable. This is because it's not going to associate with you in the proper way. The dog is going to associate that you actually screwed up its comfort and survival when you are out in public places. Therefore, it might be feeling sad or might have scared feelings or might be aggressive towards another dog because it doesn't know how to function in those situations with you.

So, don't just get a puppy and start taking it everywhere. In fact, if it's an adult dog that you have not yet socialized properly, don't just start going places. Teach that dog that you have everything to do with its survival and comfort, and then take that same mentality and behavior and routine out in public. Once the puppy gets strong enough to know who you are, then the puppy can walk through Walmart or wherever else without you having to do much.

CHAPTER 7

ACTION AND REACTION

As we've said many times, dog training tries to show the animal the quickest and best way to provide for their comfort and survival, whether that's jumping on an attacker or staying off the couch.

Everything about training a dog shows the powerful link between the dog's physical and mental being. But there is also something to be said for the technique of the trainer and the owner once the animal gets home. What you do (or don't do) has a real impact on the behavior and well-being of the animal.

For example, a puppy's idea of "uncomfortable' is beyond what we see and feel. When puppies come up to you jumping, jumping,

jumping, they're just dealing with life. They don't know what's going on. They look at you because you're something else that's in their environment. They associate that, *"If I push these buttons, I can possibly fin• comfort."* They're uncomfortable, which is why they're always barking, jumping on you, doing this and doing that.

If we allow that small bit of uncomfortable feeling to grow, then we start to create a dog that can't handle the smallest bit of discomfort. That's important to note. When we allow them to display their discomfort, which sometimes are the things we think are cute, we're actually teaching them that those feelings are the way to get what they want, rather than teaching the behaviors you want them to display. The discomfort – and the behaviors associated with it – become a means to an end.

When puppies just whine and want you to pick them up, don't do it. That's how they develop separation anxiety. Every time they felt mentally uncomfortable, they asked for your attention and you gave it to them. So, when you leave and they feel mentally uncomfortable, and you don't give them attention, they can't fathom the thought of being away from you. As a result, they might then spaz out and tear up the house. You not picking them up doesn't mean you don't love them. The key is consistency because dogs are creatures of habit. So, it shouldn't matter which human is in control of your dog at a certain time. It should just matter that someone is. Then the dog reprograms its comfort based on consistency.

I can work with my puppy, but I don't have to pick it up every time. I can be in the area of my puppy and he can be inside of a crate. If he's inside of a crate and he's whining, he doesn't come out. Once my puppy understands that he can stay in that kennel when he sees me and that I'm not always letting it out, he can form some sort of independence. And I reinforce that I have the ultimate control; I determine when that door opens.

People say, "Well, I leave my dog out at home, and he's really afraid of the refrigerator." I ask if they were there. "No, I was at work." Well, that's why. Now, you're letting your dog experience life without you. Therefore, the dog is going to be scared.

What I do is put my dog inside of a crate. If it's inside the crate around the refrigerator, it doesn't get to respond because it can't go anywhere. It's still in the crate and because of the crate, its reaction turns into "no response" to the refrigerator, which, in the dog's mind, helped it not get harmed by the refrigerator. If it was out and about and walked past the refrigerator and the ice machine went *Clunk! Clunk! Clang! Clunk!* It'd take off running. Now it's learned that, in order to survive, it has to be scared of the refrigerator because the refrigerator produced this sound that tried to harm it.

"I know it didn't kill me, but that's because I ran too fast," it thinks. "I ran away from it."

Here's another thing I hear from clients: "My dog, Scrappy Poo Pop, has too much energy. How do I drain that energy? It seems that even after long walks, he still has so much energy." That's because the energy the dog has is being conditioned through your actions of accommodating Scrappy Poo Pop every time he tells you that he needs to do something. If you let the dog out, he just wants to do zoomies. He just never gets tired. Then, he's starting to tear up things once it starts to rain outside and we're not able to go exercise.

Keep in mind, with my dog Primo, I can go to a meeting for four hours, and he would sit in an almost dreamlike state. And what's the difference between Scrappy Poo Pop and Primo? Primo has more energy than Scrappy Poo Pop (genetically), but Scrappy Poo Pop has difficulty being still. What happened to Scrappy Poo Pop was, every time he got this burst of energy, his owners took him out for a jog. Well, let's think about a pro athlete. A pro athlete wants to perform his job at the highest level of his ability. So, he conditions his body, and what does it do? It makes him stronger. It makes him conditioned.

So, a dog acts off of association. Every time it accessed that state of mind where it's all over the house and tearing up stuff, you took him for a jog. What you're doing is associating this energy with us going to go run or go play ball. Basically, you're rewarding that destructive and energetic behavior.

And that's not where it stops. Every time the dog accesses that state of mind, it takes longer and longer and longer to get tired. You've trained the dog like a pro athlete. When it throws a temper tantrum in the house, you give the dog what it wants because you take him out to run longer. It expects the action of running and, when it doesn't happen, the dog tears up the house.

People think, OK, apparently there's still some gas left in the system. I need to drive it out. After all, when I take my car out, it gets empty through the repetition of driving it. As a human, we learn that if we want to tire out our kids, we take them to the park, they run it out and they sleep like a baby. That's where we start to go wrong, thinking that dogs are the same as people.

Dogs don't associate the exact same way. If I want a dog to be calm, I have to teach the brain to be calm. The physical doesn't mean anything. People tell me if it's a really energetic dog, I bet you have a hard time. No. If, for a whole month, I didn't exercise my dog, he would be perfectly fine.

Another thing people should understand about dogs is they have a very simple philosophy when it comes to solutions to their discomfort: If it doesn't work, I'm going to stop. If it does work, I'm going to continue.

A dog has a tendency to try something different ways, multiple times to add up to whatever makes them successful. Most people don't know how a dog gets out of its kennel. The thing is, the dog tried it this way and that was one time it didn't work. So, it tried it again the same way and it didn't work. It tries it again and it doesn't work, so now the dog's brain says it doesn't work, try something else. Then, the dog tries something else about three or four times. Crossing crosses out of its mind the first and second things that did not work.

Getting a dog to do something starts with the 100-101 rule: If the dog does something incorrectly 100 times, you have to be prepared to model the correct behavior 101 times, assisted by different tools you have at your disposal, like the clicker, a corrective collar or even a simple leash.

Let's say you're trying to get the dog to stop chewing on the couch. If you put a leash on a dog and pull them away every time they try to chew up the couch, using the 100 to 101 Rule, they learn. The same goes for dogs that want to snap at other dogs. When I was training Primo and his dog aggression, I'd pull back on the leash every time he started to snap in the direction of another dog.

I should mention at this point that the timing of your correction is very, very important. Stopping a behavior means taking action when you see the dog is about to do something you don't want it to before the dog does it. Let's say I put a long lead on the dog, and if it goes to a counter and is about to jump on it, I pull the dog away from it. If it goes back, I pull it away again and then if it goes back, I pull it away again. Through repetition, that dog will learn that that mindset doesn't work. Therefore, I've been successful at discouraging the behavior and replacing it with the association that if I go to the counter, it doesn't have any outcome other than getting pulled back.

It's more about what the dog is thinking and not necessarily what the dog is doing. If my dog thinks that he wants to go over there and bite something, then I stop it from doing that. It's about making something not make sense to the dog to lose value in doing something that is not desired of him. Let's say I want my dog to stop sniffing around looking for food. Knowing by its physical signs that it's about to do that, I stop that state of mind. I don't let the dog do it. People usually spank their dogs when it bites on something. Well, the dog doesn't want to get hit, but unless it is corrected before it does something, that dog is going to continue to do it. It's about anticipation: catching the dog before the act and not in the act.

A dog is an intelligent animal. They're not a smart animal. Intelligence means that the dog will associate that every time I tried to do something that my owner didn't approve of, I was pulled back. Every time I tried to bite on the couch, I got pulled away from it. Something that simple can be processed by a dog to stop them from doing things.

Dogs exert every single possibility and that's generally what works in their favor because most humans give up before the animal does. But if you remember the 100-101 Rule, and there's not a result in the dog's favor, eventually their instinct kicks in that it lost this battle and the dog won't do anything at all.

The message you're looking to send as a dog owner to Scrappy Poo Pop is that even with all his creativity, he's not going to win. There's one way to survive, one way to find comfort, one way to act, and that's through me, the owner. Hang in there long enough, and the dog will finally just stop trying to do it their way, having been shown they have been defeated. That's a big part of the dominion that we have over the animal.

A WELL-TRAINED DOG IS AN INDEPENDENT DOG

I want to discuss the roots of separation anxiety in a little more detail, because it is the root of a lot of other negative behaviors in dogs.

When dealing with puppies, however, you convince them their lives are going to be, that's how their life is. The average person wants to pick the puppy up, love it, not let the puppy out of their sight, and so on. No matter what the puppy is doing, they give it treats, which is a very bad thing. This fools the puppy into thinking whatever it was doing at the time was enough to get food and not what you want it to do later.

In the same vein, people are too quick to respond to a puppy whining in its crate, which can become an issue. Humans sometimes don't understand how their actions affect their dog behaviors and reinforce the associations that the dog is forming.

If a puppy is crying in its crate, make sure you don't let it out. It's doing everything in its little puppy mind that it thinks it should do to freak out so that it can get closer to you. It's OK to pet puppies, but overdoing it teaches them early on that this is how life is supposed to be.

If the puppy is getting petted all of the time, and every time it jumps on you, you pick it up, then the puppy can potentially form separation anxiety. The dog realizes that you were there during every single scary moment it experienced when you're together all of the time. Now, you take yourself away to go to work, and the dog can't think, knowing that you're not around to fill those voids and those insecurities.

A dog has to learn it can be alone. It will survive and maintain a certain level of comfort. The best way to do that is to utilize the crate to limit roaming the house. If the dog is able to get to and tear up the furniture while feeling anxious, it is likely to form the association that tearing up furniture equals regaining comfort.

Leaving the dog in the crate, on the other hand, reinforces that feeling of security – being that they are able to see that whatever scares them does not harm them and limits the negative associates they are able to make. Also, the dog eventually notices its human isn't letting it out and it's not dying, so this "scary thing" is actually not harmful, that is, not affecting survival. This is what helps your dog begin to feel independent.

It all comes back to training, forming associations and consistent reinforcement. Once good habits have been established, you have to make sure that you're keeping those habits. If you don't, the dog starts to find its own ways to live life. That's what dogs worry about during times of change: *How am I going about my life now?* If the environment and situations are consistent, the dog remains consistent. If these are not consistent, then the dog changes and adapts to however it feels is the best way to survive at the time.

CHAPTER 8

THE EXPLORING MIND

In the wild, the wolf only does things that result in something meaningful. Hunting, walking, waking up, stalking, all of these are "behaviors" the animal believes will result in its survival. Like the wolf, a dog has an exploring mind and is a creature of habit. It will take the same route as a result of "behaviors" each time to get to a desired outcome. If a dog finds that route (a collective effort of behaviors) was not successful, its exploring mind has the ability to lead them to alternate routes. This is where we get into understanding why our dog chooses to listen to us or not based on our understanding of how they think.

I've been able to touch a lot of breeds in my career, and over time, I came to the realization that dogs are dogs. People ask what kind of dogs are the hardest to train. As long as it's got four legs and it barks, it's all the same.

A big part of it is proper training and socialization (or lack thereof), something you obviously cared enough about in order to buy this book. The dog's motivations and work ethic play a big part in things too – just like people, some dogs are "A students" Those students tend to be the most motivated ones.

But if you really want to know why one dog acts one way and another dog acts another way, even within the same breed, you have to look beyond just their size, strength and reputation, and look deeper into the mind.

Most people don't understand that when you are training a dog for a certain task or set of behaviors, what you're really doing is programming and training the mind. Once you do that, the physical part just follows, almost like a reflex. The dog isn't even thinking about what they are doing, because their state of mind at any given moment becomes locked into certain actions or physical movements. Change the state of mind, and you change the behavior.

I believe that all dogs, every single one, are built for a particular job, provided the mental side is shaped to match the work you want that dog to do. I have seen many dogs whose mental fitness for a given role didn't match their physical appearance. One dog that comes to mind was Big Boy, a big German shepherd I once owned. To look at him, you'd think he was the perfect candidate for protection work. We tested him out and Big Boy didn't heed anything; he just acted like the trainer wasn't there.

And why? Because at that point in my career, I didn't understand how important the mental side of training was. I trained Big Boy in a way that allowed him to be a calm, laid-back dog, believing that's how he would achieve survival and comfort. In all actuality, what I needed to instill in him from the beginning was a state of mind where protecting his owner was his only objective.

Now obviously, not all dogs are ideally suited for every job, which is why you see more German Shepherds in protection work than corgis, more Labrador retrievers in hunting than Chihuahuas, and more greyhounds in racing over an English bulldog. That's just common sense based on physical attributes. But anyone who has ever seen the small dog who doesn't know he's a small dog (or seen Spike the Doberman act like a scaredy-cat) can attest to the power of the dog's mind to control its behavior.

SUCCESS LIES IN THE SKULL

I learned from the mistakes I made with Big Boy and hundreds of others (and yes, I've really owned hundreds of dogs in my lifetime). Today, training the dog's mind is the main focus of my training methodology, and I have thousands of satisfied customers and happy, well-adjusted dogs to show for it. This is not only important in general, but is an important technique in addressing specific behavioral problems.

Let's say I encounter a puppy that is naturally aggressive. The first and most important lesson that a puppy has to learn is that I'm in control. Since I am the source of its survival (food) and comfort, the puppy quickly understands that it needs to adopt new behaviors.

Remember what we said before: Dogs are practical. They only perform an action that produces a reward. When a dog believes in its mind that what it is doing either isn't getting anywhere or there's a consequence for it, the dog will change its behavior.

That's how I am able to take a fighting pitbull and train this dog to where it can now focus on me instead of other dogs in the environment. The dog loves people, but to a person, people say it's ingrained in that dog to fight, to be aggressive. That's not true. When I get the dog to view me as the Alpha, there's no fighting going on here or hard feelings. The dogs are not allowed to feel this way because there's a consequence for it, and it doesn't help them at all.

It works in reverse, too. Whether a dog is showing defiant behavior or good behavior, both of those can be altered through mental conditioning. It doesn't matter how good a dog is or how happy it is to be around people. When a person performs repetitive actions, the dog soon learns how to react a certain way towards people, even if he is a good dog.

Is that the dog's fault? Most people would say no, but at the moment, they generally blame the dog's breed as being naturally aggressive. It's not necessarily the breed itself. It's how you raise it and shape it to become the dog that you want that really counts.

A dog's energy is due to their exploring mind. When their mind is in a curious state, the dog learns through repetition to continue certain behaviors, which increases the creativity of their exploring mind. This is what people who think having the dog exercise is the solution to tire them out gets wrong. If the dog is in an exploring state, that is the time to exercise the mind and not the body. The downfall of conditioning the dog's body is that they just become stronger, and you, the owner, are just creating more work for yourself.

THE LAST PIECE TO THE PUZZLE

Every time we return a dog to its owner after its training has been completed, I always have the same nervous feeling in my stomach. It doesn't have anything to do with the animal, but whether or not the owner will continue to keep up the skills learned. I'm always thinking, "*I hope they are ready for this.*"

In a very short period of time, I have come to know the dog very well and can see what the animal's tendencies and habits are. I know its personality, and I know the buttons to push to get the behavior I want. If that dog were to live with me forever, I can see the kind of life it would have.

The single biggest reason for a well-trained dog to fail in their conditioning doesn't have anything to do with age, breed or the size of the owner's house or bank account. But it has everything to do with the ability of that owner to continue the work we have started.

This has been a difficulty I have had to face in my business. I know I am good at training, but it's only been in the last few years that I have been equally good at relaying messages to the owners so that they understand how training works and their role in their dog's success. Sometimes they get it, and the results are phenomenal; a lot of times they don't and the dog goes right back to where they started from or worse.

Here are a few key points to remember *after* the trainer leaves.

1. **Consistency is key.** If I dropped off Primo (or any of the highly-trained dogs I've worked with over the years) and the new owner understood and handled him as I did, that dog wouldn't care at all about me. He's getting what he needs for survival and comfort from the owner, and that's fine with him. It's "Calvin who?" at that point.

   But if reinforcement is not consistent, it gives the dog the opportunity to push the envelope and do certain things that convince it that it doesn't need the owner for survival or comfort. Once that happens, the dog is calling the shots, not you.

2. **Mind your mojo.** Dogs can instinctually read energy which helps them avoid danger and size up other living things. People give off different energies, the same way that a lion and a rabbit do and the dog reacts accordingly. I've trained super nice dogs that go to another home and develop dog aggression. That dog wouldn't have formed those feelings of aggression under my care.

The relationship changed because the owner didn't reinforce their position as the alpha.

I taught the dog that its survival relies on my energy. If the owner doesn't demonstrate the same energy, the dog doesn't feel like it's safe without me there. So, it reacts accordingly. If being aggressive helps the dog's mindset in that situation, then it thinks that being aggressive will help it survive and be comfortable going forward.

3. **There is no off-season.** I train dogs for a living. Because of that, I give what I do my full attention at all times. I'm constantly reading the dogs I am working with. If you've ever seen my eyes around a dog, I'm just locked in and focused. If I don't, then something else will take my place to shape the dog's behavior.

    For example, previous experience has taught me dogs train other dogs. So, when I put dogs together, I'm focusing on every little muscle that moves when they walk, every behavior that they display. If I see that a dog is about to get upset, I immediately stop the thought process.

    As a dog owner, you're in the same boat. You have to constantly pay attention and reinforce good behaviors (as well as proactively stop bad ones), especially when dealing with potentially destructive behaviors.

4. **Take accountability.** People train dogs without knowing it. Every dog that has a behavior problem has had outside influences to develop that problem, and 99 times out of 100, that influence

comes in some form or fashion from the owner. They just didn't know that they were doing it.

It's not the wrong puppy. It's not the nature of the breed. A dog will show certain tendencies and habits that they can develop by accident, but those tendencies become a habit because of the owner. A dog's brain can be altered through reinforcement consistent enough to where the dog forms a habit. I've seen a puppy that has nice tendencies and attributes and a super cool demeanor turn aggressive because the owner was not consistent. You're basically allowing your lifestyle to train the dog and not you at that point. Without you knowing, that's what you're doing.

Thanks for taking the time to understand your dog better!

Made in the USA
Columbia, SC
12 May 2022